D1636548

Gratitude Journal

This journal belongs to

_____

gratitude

grat·i·tude | \ ˈgra-tə-ˌtüd , -ˌtyüd \
: a feeling of appreciation or thanks

Gratitude, thankfulness or gratefulness, from the Latin word *gratus* "pleasing, thankful", is a feeling of appreciation felt by recipient for positivity, kindness, gifts, help,favors, or other type of generosity that is received.

Gratitude is a state of being – a state of thankfulness that allow you to reminisce and be thankful for all that you have in your lif and brings about a positive state of mind. It's about focusing o what's good in your life and being thankful for the things yo have. It is about taking pause and appreciating the things tha may be taken for granted such as family, friends, food, clea water and a place to live.

Research has suggested that people who are more grateful ar happier, less depressed, less stressed, and more satisfied wit their lives and social relationships. They are found to be mor joyful in the long term.

Grateful people have also been found to have a higher level control of their environments, personal growth, purpose in lif and self acceptance. They are more likely to seek positive ways coping with the difficulties they experience in life and grow fro experiences.
Practicing gratitude at the beginning of the day sets the tone fo the whole day.

habit

hab·it | \ ˈha-bət \
: a settled tendency or usual manner of
: an acquired mode of behavior that has become
nearly or completely involuntary

It has been found that it takes 21 days to create a habit and 90 days to make it a part of your lifestyle.

This 21/90 formula was brought to light in 1960, when a cosmetic surgeon named Dr Maxwell Maltz wrote a self-help book called *Psycho Cybernetics, A New Way to Get More Living Out of Life*.

It is a brilliant way to form good habits which in turn bring about a happy, positive, healthy lifestyle!

And with that lets begin our journey!

Daily Habits

☐ Make your bed – First task of the day done!

☐ Drink a big glass of water – You've dehydrated while sleeping; quench your thirst!

☐ Stretch – Lengthen and loosen your body; it has been still for awhile!

☐ 5 minutes of physical activity – Get your blood pumping and your mind refreshed!

☐ 5 minutes of meditation – Focus on your breath and set your intentions for the day!

☐ Read for 5 minutes – Expand your knowledge!

☐ Make a 'To Do List' – What would you like to accomplish today?

☐ Gratitude - What are you grateful for today?

TO DO LIST:

_____   _____

_____   _____

_____   _____

_____   _____

_____   _____

Believe in yourself and anything is possible!!

I am Grateful For:

_____
_____
_____
_____
_____
_____
_____
_____
_____
_____
_____
_____
_____
_____
_____
_____
_____
_____
_____
_____
_____
_____

Daily Habits

☐ Make your bed – First task of the day done!

☐ Drink a big glass of water – You've dehydrated while sleeping; quench your thirst!

☐ Stretch – Lengthen and loosen your body; it has been still for awhile!

☐ 5 minutes of physical activity – Get your blood pumping and your mind refreshed!

☐ 5 minutes of meditation – Focus on your breath and set your intentions for the day!

☐ Read for 5 minutes – Expand your knowledge!

☐ Make a 'To Do List' – What would you like to accomplish today?

☐ Gratitude - What are you grateful for today?

TO DO LIST:

_____   _____

_____   _____

_____   _____

_____   _____

_____   _____

Dare to push yourself harder today!

I am Grateful For:

_____

_____

_____

_____

_____

_____

_____

_____

_____

_____

_____

_____

_____

_____

_____

_____

_____

_____

_____

Daily Habits

☐ Make your bed – First task of the day done!

☐ Drink a big glass of water – You've dehydrated while sleeping; quench your thirst!

☐ Stretch – Lengthen and loosen your body; it has been still for awhile!

☐ 5 minutes of physical activity – Get your blood pumping and your mind refreshed!

☐ 5 minutes of meditation – Focus on your breath and set your intentions for the day!

☐ Read for 5 minutes – Expand your knowledge!

☐ Make a 'To Do List' – What would you like to accomplish today?

☐ Gratitude - What are you grateful for today?

TO DO LIST:

_____   _____

_____   _____

_____   _____

_____   _____

_____   _____

One Life....Seize it!!

I am Grateful For:

_____

_____

_____

_____

_____

_____

_____

_____

_____

_____

_____

_____

_____

_____

_____

_____

_____

_____

_____

_____

_____

Daily Habits

☐ Make your bed – First task of the day done!

☐ Drink a big glass of water – You've dehydrated while sleeping; quench your thirst!

☐ Stretch – Lengthen and loosen your body; it has been still for awhile!

☐ 5 minutes of physical activity – Get your blood pumping and your mind refreshed!

☐ 5 minutes of meditation – Focus on your breath and set your intentions for the day!

☐ Read for 5 minutes – Expand your knowledge!

☐ Make a 'To Do List' – What would you like to accomplish today?

☐ Gratitude - What are you grateful for today?

TO DO LIST:

_____   _____

_____   _____

_____   _____

_____   _____

_____   _____

Captivate them!!

I am Grateful For:

_____
_____
_____
_____
_____
_____
_____
_____
_____
_____
_____
_____
_____
_____
_____
_____
_____
_____
_____
_____
_____
_____
_____
_____
_____
_____

Daily Habits

- ☐ Make your bed – First task of the day done!

- ☐ Drink a big glass of water – You've dehydrated while sleeping; quench your thirst!

- ☐ Stretch – Lengthen and loosen your body; it has been still for awhile!

- ☐ 5 minutes of physical activity – Get your blood pumping and your mind refreshed!

- ☐ 5 minutes of meditation – Focus on your breath and set your intentions for the day!

- ☐ Read for 5 minutes – Expand your knowledge!

- ☐ Make a 'To Do List' – What would you like to accomplish today?

- ☐ Gratitude - What are you grateful for today?

TO DO LIST:

_____   _____

_____   _____

_____   _____

_____   _____

_____   _____

You are Unstoppable!!

I am Grateful For:

_____

_____

_____

_____

_____

_____

_____

_____

_____

_____

_____

_____

_____

_____

_____

_____

_____

_____

_____

_____

_____

<u>Daily Habits</u>

- ☐ Make your bed – First task of the day done!

- ☐ Drink a big glass of water – You've dehydrated while sleeping; quench your thirst!

- ☐ Stretch – Lengthen and loosen your body; it has been still for awhile!

- ☐ 5 minutes of physical activity – Get your blood pumping and your mind refreshed!

- ☐ 5 minutes of meditation – Focus on your breath and set your intentions for the day!

- ☐ Read for 5 minutes – Expand your knowledge!

- ☐ Make a 'To Do List' – What would you like to accomplish today?

- ☐ Gratitude - What are you grateful for today?

TO DO LIST:

_____   _____

_____   _____

_____   _____

_____   _____

_____   _____

Do it because you Love it!

I am Grateful For:

_____

_____

_____

_____

_____

_____

_____

_____

_____

_____

_____

_____

_____

_____

_____

_____

_____

_____

_____

_____

"When you look at life through the eyes of gratitude, the world becomes a magical and amazing place."

– Jennifer Gayle

REFLECTIONS:

Daily Habits

☐ Make your bed – First task of the day done!

☐ Drink a big glass of water – You've dehydrated while sleeping; quench your thirst!

☐ Stretch – Lengthen and loosen your body; it has been still for awhile!

☐ 5 minutes of physical activity – Get your blood pumping and your mind refreshed!

☐ 5 minutes of meditation – Focus on your breath and set your intentions for the day!

☐ Read for 5 minutes – Expand your knowledge!

☐ Make a 'To Do List' – What would you like to accomplish today?

☐ Gratitude - What are you grateful for today?

TO DO LIST:

_____   _____

_____   _____

_____   _____

_____   _____

_____   _____

Don't be Afraid to Fail….Be afraid to not try!

I am Grateful For:

_____

_____

_____

_____

_____

_____

_____

_____

_____

_____

_____

_____

_____

_____

_____

_____

_____

_____

_____

_____

_____

_____

_____

_____

Daily Habits

☐ Make your bed – First task of the day done!

☐ Drink a big glass of water – You've dehydrated while sleeping; quench your thirst!

☐ Stretch – Lengthen and loosen your body; it has been still for awhile!

☐ 5 minutes of physical activity – Get your blood pumping and your mind refreshed!

☐ 5 minutes of meditation – Focus on your breath and set your intentions for the day!

☐ Read for 5 minutes – Expand your knowledge!

☐ Make a 'To Do List' – What would you like to accomplish today?

☐ Gratitude - What are you grateful for today?

TO DO LIST:

_____   _____

_____   _____

_____   _____

_____   _____

_____   _____

You can do anything you set your mind to!

I am Grateful For:

_____

_____

_____

_____

_____

_____

_____

_____

_____

_____

_____

_____

_____

_____

_____

_____

_____

_____

_____

_____

Daily Habits

- [ ] Make your bed – First task of the day done!

- [ ] Drink a big glass of water – You've dehydrated while sleeping; quench your thirst!

- [ ] Stretch – Lengthen and loosen your body; it has been still for awhile!

- [ ] 5 minutes of physical activity – Get your blood pumping and your mind refreshed!

- [ ] 5 minutes of meditation – Focus on your breath and set your intentions for the day!

- [ ] Read for 5 minutes – Expand your knowledge!

- [ ] Make a 'To Do List' – What would you like to accomplish today?

- [ ] Gratitude - What are you grateful for today?

TO DO LIST:

_____   _____

_____   _____

_____   _____

_____   _____

_____   _____

Every journey begins with the first step!

I am Grateful For:

_____

_____

_____

_____

_____

_____

_____

_____

_____

_____

_____

_____

_____

_____

_____

_____

_____

_____

_____

_____

<u>Daily Habits</u>

- ☐ Make your bed – First task of the day done!

- ☐ Drink a big glass of water – You've dehydrated while sleeping; quench your thirst!

- ☐ Stretch – Lengthen and loosen your body; it has been still for awhile!

- ☐ 5 minutes of physical activity – Get your blood pumping and your mind refreshed!

- ☐ 5 minutes of meditation – Focus on your breath and set your intentions for the day!

- ☐ Read for 5 minutes – Expand your knowledge!

- ☐ Make a 'To Do List' – What would you like to accomplish today?

- ☐ Gratitude - What are you grateful for today?

TO DO LIST:

_____   _____

_____   _____

_____   _____

_____   _____

_____   _____

The question isn't who is going to let you, it's who is going to stop you!

I am Grateful For:

_____

_____

_____

_____

_____

_____

_____

_____

_____

_____

_____

_____

_____

_____

_____

_____

_____

_____

_____

Daily Habits

☐ Make your bed – First task of the day done!

☐ Drink a big glass of water – You've dehydrated while sleeping; quench your thirst!

☐ Stretch – Lengthen and loosen your body; it has been still for awhile!

☐ 5 minutes of physical activity – Get your blood pumping and your mind refreshed!

☐ 5 minutes of meditation – Focus on your breath and set your intentions for the day!

☐ Read for 5 minutes – Expand your knowledge!

☐ Make a 'To Do List' – What would you like to accomplish today?

☐ Gratitude - What are you grateful for today?

TO DO LIST:

_____   _____

_____   _____

_____   _____

_____   _____

_____   _____

A beautiful day starts with a beautiful mindset!

I am Grateful For:

_____

_____

_____

_____

_____

_____

_____

_____

_____

_____

_____

_____

_____

_____

_____

_____

_____

_____

_____

Daily Habits

☐ Make your bed – First task of the day done!

☐ Drink a big glass of water – You've dehydrated while sleeping; quench your thirst!

☐ Stretch – Lengthen and loosen your body; it has been still for awhile!

☐ 5 minutes of physical activity – Get your blood pumping and your mind refreshed!

☐ 5 minutes of meditation – Focus on your breath and set your intentions for the day!

☐ Read for 5 minutes – Expand your knowledge!

☐ Make a 'To Do List' – What would you like to accomplish today?

☐ Gratitude - What are you grateful for today?

TO DO LIST:

_____   _____

_____   _____

_____   _____

_____   _____

_____   _____

Push yourself to be the best version of you!

I am Grateful For:

_____

_____

_____

_____

_____

_____

_____

_____

_____

_____

_____

_____

_____

_____

_____

_____

_____

_____

_____

_____

Daily Habits

☐ Make your bed – First task of the day done!

☐ Drink a big glass of water – You've dehydrated while sleeping; quench your thirst!

☐ Stretch – Lengthen and loosen your body; it has been still for awhile!

☐ 5 minutes of physical activity – Get your blood pumping and your mind refreshed!

☐ 5 minutes of meditation – Focus on your breath and set your intentions for the day!

☐ Read for 5 minutes – Expand your knowledge!

☐ Make a 'To Do List' – What would you like to accomplish today?

☐ Gratitude - What are you grateful for today?

TO DO LIST:

_____   _____

_____   _____

_____   _____

_____   _____

_____   _____

You can do anything!

I am Grateful For:

_____
_____
_____
_____
_____
_____
_____
_____
_____
_____
_____
_____
_____
_____
_____
_____
_____
_____
_____
_____
_____
_____
_____
_____

Daily Habits

☐ Make your bed – First task of the day done!

☐ Drink a big glass of water – You've dehydrated while sleeping; quench your thirst!

☐ Stretch – Lengthen and loosen your body; it has been still for awhile!

☐ 5 minutes of physical activity – Get your blood pumping and your mind refreshed!

☐ 5 minutes of meditation – Focus on your breath and set your intentions for the day!

☐ Read for 5 minutes – Expand your knowledge!

☐ Make a 'To Do List' – What would you like to accomplish today?

☐ Gratitude - What are you grateful for today?

TO DO LIST:

_____   _____

_____   _____

_____   _____

_____   _____

_____   _____

Every day is a chance to be better!

I am Grateful For:

_____

_____

_____

_____

_____

_____

_____

_____

_____

_____

_____

_____

_____

_____

_____

_____

_____

_____

_____

_____

Daily Habits

- ☐ Make your bed – First task of the day done!

- ☐ Drink a big glass of water – You've dehydrated while sleeping; quench your thirst!

- ☐ Stretch – Lengthen and loosen your body; it has been still for awhile!

- ☐ 5 minutes of physical activity – Get your blood pumping and your mind refreshed!

- ☐ 5 minutes of meditation – Focus on your breath and set your intentions for the day!

- ☐ Read for 5 minutes – Expand your knowledge!

- ☐ Make a 'To Do List' – What would you like to accomplish today?

- ☐ Gratitude - What are you grateful for today?

TO DO LIST:

_____   _____

_____   _____

_____   _____

_____   _____

_____   _____

Chase your dreams!

I am Grateful For:

_____
_____
_____
_____
_____
_____
_____
_____
_____
_____
_____
_____
_____
_____
_____
_____
_____
_____
_____
_____
_____
_____
_____

Daily Habits

- ☐ Make your bed – First task of the day done!

- ☐ Drink a big glass of water – You've dehydrated while sleeping; quench your thirst!

- ☐ Stretch – Lengthen and loosen your body; it has been still for awhile!

- ☐ 5 minutes of physical activity – Get your blood pumping and your mind refreshed!

- ☐ 5 minutes of meditation – Focus on your breath and set your intentions for the day!

- ☐ Read for 5 minutes – Expand your knowledge!

- ☐ Make a 'To Do List' – What would you like to accomplish today?

- ☐ Gratitude - What are you grateful for today?

TO DO LIST:

_____   _____

_____   _____

_____   _____

_____   _____

_____   _____

Believe you can and you're halfway there – Theodore Roosevelt

I am Grateful For:

_____

_____

_____

_____

_____

_____

_____

_____

_____

_____

_____

_____

_____

_____

_____

_____

_____

_____

_____

_____

_____

<u>Daily Habits</u>

- ☐ Make your bed – First task of the day done!

- ☐ Drink a big glass of water – You've dehydrated while sleeping; quench your thirst!

- ☐ Stretch – Lengthen and loosen your body; it has been still for awhile!

- ☐ 5 minutes of physical activity – Get your blood pumping and your mind refreshed!

- ☐ 5 minutes of meditation – Focus on your breath and set your intentions for the day!

- ☐ Read for 5 minutes – Expand your knowledge!

- ☐ Make a 'To Do List' – What would you like to accomplish today?

- ☐ Gratitude - What are you grateful for today?

TO DO LIST:

_____   _____

_____   _____

_____   _____

_____   _____

_____   _____

Today is another day to make your dreams come true!!

I am Grateful For:

_____

_____

_____

_____

_____

_____

_____

_____

_____

_____

_____

_____

_____

_____

_____

_____

_____

_____

Daily Habits

☐ Make your bed – First task of the day done!

☐ Drink a big glass of water – You've dehydrated while sleeping; quench your thirst!

☐ Stretch – Lengthen and loosen your body; it has been still for awhile!

☐ 5 minutes of physical activity – Get your blood pumping and your mind refreshed!

☐ 5 minutes of meditation – Focus on your breath and set your intentions for the day!

☐ Read for 5 minutes – Expand your knowledge!

☐ Make a 'To Do List' – What would you like to accomplish today?

☐ Gratitude - What are you grateful for today?

TO DO LIST:

_____   _____

_____   _____

_____   _____

_____   _____

_____   _____

You're One of a kind!

I am Grateful For:

_____

_____

_____

_____

_____

_____

_____

_____

_____

_____

_____

_____

_____

_____

_____

_____

_____

_____

_____

_____

_____

_____

_____

> *"The single greatest thing you can do to change your life today would be to start being grateful for what you have right now."*
>
> – Oprah Winfrey

REFLECTIONS:

Daily Habits

- ☐ Make your bed – First task of the day done!

- ☐ Drink a big glass of water – You've dehydrated while sleeping; quench your thirst!

- ☐ Stretch – Lengthen and loosen your body; it has been still for awhile!

- ☐ 5 minutes of physical activity – Get your blood pumping and your mind refreshed!

- ☐ 5 minutes of meditation – Focus on your breath and set your intentions for the day!

- ☐ Read for 5 minutes – Expand your knowledge!

- ☐ Make a 'To Do List' – What would you like to accomplish today?

- ☐ Gratitude - What are you grateful for today?

TO DO LIST:

_____   _____

_____   _____

_____   _____

_____   _____

_____   _____

Don't limit your challenges; challenge your limits!

I am Grateful For:

_____

_____

_____

_____

_____

_____

_____

_____

_____

_____

_____

_____

_____

_____

_____

_____

_____

_____

_____

_____

Daily Habits

☐ Make your bed – First task of the day done!

☐ Drink a big glass of water – You've dehydrated while sleeping; quench your thirst!

☐ Stretch – Lengthen and loosen your body; it has been still for awhile!

☐ 5 minutes of physical activity – Get your blood pumping and your mind refreshed!

☐ 5 minutes of meditation – Focus on your breath and set your intentions for the day!

☐ Read for 5 minutes – Expand your knowledge!

☐ Make a 'To Do List' – What would you like to accomplish today?

☐ Gratitude - What are you grateful for today?

TO DO LIST:

_____   _____

_____   _____

_____   _____

_____   _____

_____   _____

Dream it. Believe it. Achieve it!

I am Grateful For:

_____

_____

_____

_____

_____

_____

_____

_____

_____

_____

_____

_____

_____

_____

_____

_____

_____

_____

_____

_____

_____

Daily Habits

- ☐ Make your bed – First task of the day done!

- ☐ Drink a big glass of water – You've dehydrated while sleeping; quench your thirst!

- ☐ Stretch – Lengthen and loosen your body; it has been still for awhile!

- ☐ 5 minutes of physical activity – Get your blood pumping and your mind refreshed!

- ☐ 5 minutes of meditation – Focus on your breath and set your intentions for the day!

- ☐ Read for 5 minutes – Expand your knowledge!

- ☐ Make a 'To Do List' – What would you like to accomplish today?

- ☐ Gratitude - What are you grateful for today?

TO DO LIST:

_____   _____

_____   _____

_____   _____

_____   _____

_____   _____

Don't stop until you're proud!

I am Grateful For:

_____

_____

_____

_____

_____

_____

_____

_____

_____

_____

_____

_____

_____

_____

_____

_____

_____

_____

_____

_____

Daily Habits

☐ Make your bed – First task of the day done!

☐ Drink a big glass of water – You've dehydrated while sleeping; quench your thirst!

☐ Stretch – Lengthen and loosen your body; it has been still for awhile!

☐ 5 minutes of physical activity – Get your blood pumping and your mind refreshed!

☐ 5 minutes of meditation – Focus on your breath and set your intentions for the day!

☐ Read for 5 minutes – Expand your knowledge!

☐ Make a 'To Do List' – What would you like to accomplish today?

☐ Gratitude - What are you grateful for today?

TO DO LIST:

_____   _____

_____   _____

_____   _____

_____   _____

_____   _____

Life is so much brighter when we focus on what truly matters!

I am Grateful For:

_____

_____

_____

_____

_____

_____

_____

_____

_____

_____

_____

_____

_____

_____

_____

_____

_____

_____

_____

_____

Daily Habits

- ☐ Make your bed – First task of the day done!

- ☐ Drink a big glass of water – You've dehydrated while sleeping; quench your thirst!

- ☐ Stretch – Lengthen and loosen your body; it has been still for awhile!

- ☐ 5 minutes of physical activity – Get your blood pumping and your mind refreshed!

- ☐ 5 minutes of meditation – Focus on your breath and set your intentions for the day!

- ☐ Read for 5 minutes – Expand your knowledge!

- ☐ Make a 'To Do List' – What would you like to accomplish today?

- ☐ Gratitude - What are you grateful for today?

TO DO LIST:

_____   _____

_____   _____

_____   _____

_____   _____

_____   _____

If you are always trying to be normal you will never know how amazing you can be!

I am Grateful For:

_____
_____
_____
_____
_____
_____
_____
_____
_____
_____
_____
_____
_____
_____
_____
_____
_____
_____
_____
_____
_____
_____

Daily Habits

☐ Make your bed – First task of the day done!

☐ Drink a big glass of water – You've dehydrated while sleeping; quench your thirst!

☐ Stretch – Lengthen and loosen your body; it has been still for awhile!

☐ 5 minutes of physical activity – Get your blood pumping and your mind refreshed!

☐ 5 minutes of meditation – Focus on your breath and set your intentions for the day!

☐ Read for 5 minutes – Expand your knowledge!

☐ Make a 'To Do List' – What would you like to accomplish today?

☐ Gratitude - What are you grateful for today?

TO DO LIST:

_____   _____

_____   _____

_____   _____

_____   _____

_____   _____

Make them stop and stare!!

I am Grateful For:

_____

_____

_____

_____

_____

_____

_____

_____

_____

_____

_____

_____

_____

_____

_____

_____

_____

_____

_____

_____

_____

_____

_____

Daily Habits

☐ Make your bed – First task of the day done!

☐ Drink a big glass of water – You've dehydrated while sleeping; quench your thirst!

☐ Stretch – Lengthen and loosen your body; it has been still for awhile!

☐ 5 minutes of physical activity – Get your blood pumping and your mind refreshed!

☐ 5 minutes of meditation – Focus on your breath and set your intentions for the day!

☐ Read for 5 minutes – Expand your knowledge!

☐ Make a 'To Do List' – What would you like to accomplish today?

☐ Gratitude - What are you grateful for today?

TO DO LIST:

_____   _____

_____   _____

_____   _____

_____   _____

_____   _____

Rise and Slay!!

I am Grateful For:

_____

_____

_____

_____

_____

_____

_____

_____

_____

_____

_____

_____

_____

_____

_____

_____

_____

_____

_____

_____

_____

Daily Habits

- ☐ Make your bed – First task of the day done!

- ☐ Drink a big glass of water – You've dehydrated while sleeping; quench your thirst!

- ☐ Stretch – Lengthen and loosen your body; it has been still for awhile!

- ☐ 5 minutes of physical activity – Get your blood pumping and your mind refreshed!

- ☐ 5 minutes of meditation – Focus on your breath and set your intentions for the day!

- ☐ Read for 5 minutes – Expand your knowledge!

- ☐ Make a 'To Do List' – What would you like to accomplish today?

- ☐ Gratitude - What are you grateful for today?

TO DO LIST:

_____   _____

_____   _____

_____   _____

_____   _____

_____   _____

If you aren't willing to work for it; you won't achieve it!

I am Grateful For:

_____

_____

_____

_____

_____

_____

_____

_____

_____

_____

_____

_____

_____

_____

_____

_____

_____

_____

_____

_____

Daily Habits

☐ Make your bed – First task of the day done!

☐ Drink a big glass of water – You've dehydrated while sleeping; quench your thirst!

☐ Stretch – Lengthen and loosen your body; it has been still for awhile!

☐ 5 minutes of physical activity – Get your blood pumping and your mind refreshed!

☐ 5 minutes of meditation – Focus on your breath and set your intentions for the day!

☐ Read for 5 minutes – Expand your knowledge!

☐ Make a 'To Do List' – What would you like to accomplish today?

☐ Gratitude - What are you grateful for today?

TO DO LIST:

_____   _____

_____   _____

_____   _____

_____   _____

_____   _____

Your only limit is you!!

I am Grateful For:

_____
_____
_____
_____
_____
_____
_____
_____
_____
_____
_____
_____
_____
_____
_____
_____
_____
_____
_____
_____
_____

Daily Habits

☐   Make your bed – First task of the day done!

☐   Drink a big glass of water – You've dehydrated while sleeping; quench your thirst!

☐   Stretch – Lengthen and loosen your body; it has been still for awhile!

☐   5 minutes of physical activity – Get your blood pumping and your mind refreshed!

☐   5 minutes of meditation – Focus on your breath and set your intentions for the day!

☐   Read for 5 minutes – Expand your knowledge!

☐   Make a 'To Do List' – What would you like to accomplish today?

☐   Gratitude - What are you grateful for today?

TO DO LIST:

_____	_____
_____	_____
_____	_____
_____	_____
_____	_____

Fill today with gratitude!

I am Grateful For:

_____

_____

_____

_____

_____

_____

_____

_____

_____

_____

_____

_____

_____

_____

_____

_____

_____

_____

_____

_____

_____

_____

Daily Habits

- ☐ Make your bed – First task of the day done!

- ☐ Drink a big glass of water – You've dehydrated while sleeping; quench your thirst!

- ☐ Stretch – Lengthen and loosen your body; it has been still for awhile!

- ☐ 5 minutes of physical activity – Get your blood pumping and your mind refreshed!

- ☐ 5 minutes of meditation – Focus on your breath and set your intentions for the day!

- ☐ Read for 5 minutes – Expand your knowledge!

- ☐ Make a 'To Do List' – What would you like to accomplish today?

- ☐ Gratitude - What are you grateful for today?

TO DO LIST:

_____   _____

_____   _____

_____   _____

_____   _____

_____   _____

Create your sunshine!

I am Grateful For:

_____

_____

_____

_____

_____

_____

_____

_____

_____

_____

_____

_____

_____

_____

_____

_____

_____

_____

_____

_____

Daily Habits

☐ Make your bed – First task of the day done!

☐ Drink a big glass of water – You've dehydrated while sleeping; quench your thirst!

☐ Stretch – Lengthen and loosen your body; it has been still for awhile!

☐ 5 minutes of physical activity – Get your blood pumping and your mind refreshed!

☐ 5 minutes of meditation – Focus on your breath and set your intentions for the day!

☐ Read for 5 minutes – Expand your knowledge!

☐ Make a 'To Do List' – What would you like to accomplish today?

☐ Gratitude - What are you grateful for today?

TO DO LIST:

_____   _____

_____   _____

_____   _____

_____   _____

_____   _____

Make each day your Masterpiece – John Wooden

I am Grateful For:

_____
_____
_____
_____
_____
_____
_____
_____
_____
_____
_____
_____
_____
_____
_____
_____
_____
_____
_____
_____
_____
_____

"*Gratitude is a powerful process for shifting your energy and bringing more of what you want into your life. Be grateful for what you already have and you will attract more good things.*"

– Rhonda Byrne

REFLECTIONS:

<u>Daily Habits</u>

- ☐ Make your bed – First task of the day done!

- ☐ Drink a big glass of water – You've dehydrated while sleeping; quench your thirst!

- ☐ Stretch – Lengthen and loosen your body; it has been still for awhile!

- ☐ 5 minutes of physical activity – Get your blood pumping and your mind refreshed!

- ☐ 5 minutes of meditation – Focus on your breath and set your intentions for the day!

- ☐ Read for 5 minutes – Expand your knowledge!

- ☐ Make a 'To Do List' – What would you like to accomplish today?

- ☐ Gratitude - What are you grateful for today?

TO DO LIST:

_____   _____

_____   _____

_____   _____

_____   _____

_____   _____

Life is much brighter when you focus on what truly matters!

I am Grateful For:

_____

_____

_____

_____

_____

_____

_____

_____

_____

_____

_____

_____

_____

_____

_____

_____

_____

_____

_____

_____

_____

Daily Habits

☐ Make your bed – First task of the day done!

☐ Drink a big glass of water – You've dehydrated while sleeping; quench your thirst!

☐ Stretch – Lengthen and loosen your body; it has been still for awhile!

☐ 5 minutes of physical activity – Get your blood pumping and your mind refreshed!

☐ 5 minutes of meditation – Focus on your breath and set your intentions for the day!

☐ Read for 5 minutes – Expand your knowledge!

☐ Make a 'To Do List' – What would you like to accomplish today?

☐ Gratitude - What are you grateful for today?

TO DO LIST:

_____   _____

_____   _____

_____   _____

_____   _____

_____   _____

Make it happen!

I am Grateful For:

_____

_____

_____

_____

_____

_____

_____

_____

_____

_____

_____

_____

_____

_____

_____

_____

_____

_____

_____

_____

_____

_____

Daily Habits

- ☐ Make your bed – First task of the day done!

- ☐ Drink a big glass of water – You've dehydrated while sleeping; quench your thirst!

- ☐ Stretch – Lengthen and loosen your body; it has been still for awhile!

- ☐ 5 minutes of physical activity – Get your blood pumping and your mind refreshed!

- ☐ 5 minutes of meditation – Focus on your breath and set your intentions for the day!

- ☐ Read for 5 minutes – Expand your knowledge!

- ☐ Make a 'To Do List' – What would you like to accomplish today?

- ☐ Gratitude - What are you grateful for today?

TO DO LIST:

_____   _____

_____   _____

_____   _____

_____   _____

_____   _____

Don't wait for an opportunity. Create it!

I am Grateful For:

_____

_____

_____

_____

_____

_____

_____

_____

_____

_____

_____

_____

_____

_____

_____

_____

_____

_____

_____

_____

Daily Habits

- ☐ Make your bed – First task of the day done!

- ☐ Drink a big glass of water – You've dehydrated while sleeping; quench your thirst!

- ☐ Stretch – Lengthen and loosen your body; it has been still for awhile!

- ☐ 5 minutes of physical activity – Get your blood pumping and your mind refreshed!

- ☐ 5 minutes of meditation – Focus on your breath and set your intentions for the day!

- ☐ Read for 5 minutes – Expand your knowledge!

- ☐ Make a 'To Do List' – What would you like to accomplish today?

- ☐ Gratitude - What are you grateful for today?

TO DO LIST:

_____   _____

_____   _____

_____   _____

_____   _____

_____   _____

Work Hard, Dream Big and Never Give up!!

I am Grateful For:

_____
_____
_____
_____
_____
_____
_____
_____
_____
_____
_____
_____
_____
_____
_____
_____
_____
_____
_____
_____
_____
_____

Daily Habits

- ☐ Make your bed – First task of the day done!

- ☐ Drink a big glass of water – You've dehydrated while sleeping; quench your thirst!

- ☐ Stretch – Lengthen and loosen your body; it has been still for awhile!

- ☐ 5 minutes of physical activity – Get your blood pumping and your mind refreshed!

- ☐ 5 minutes of meditation – Focus on your breath and set your intentions for the day!

- ☐ Read for 5 minutes – Expand your knowledge!

- ☐ Make a 'To Do List' – What would you like to accomplish today?

- ☐ Gratitude - What are you grateful for today?

TO DO LIST:

_____   _____

_____   _____

_____   _____

_____   _____

_____   _____

Actually; you can!

I am Grateful For:

_____
_____
_____
_____
_____
_____
_____
_____
_____
_____
_____
_____
_____
_____
_____
_____
_____
_____
_____
_____
_____
_____
_____
_____
_____
_____
_____

Daily Habits

☐ Make your bed – First task of the day done!

☐ Drink a big glass of water – You've dehydrated while sleeping; quench your thirst!

☐ Stretch – Lengthen and loosen your body; it has been still for awhile!

☐ 5 minutes of physical activity – Get your blood pumping and your mind refreshed!

☐ 5 minutes of meditation – Focus on your breath and set your intentions for the day!

☐ Read for 5 minutes – Expand your knowledge!

☐ Make a 'To Do List' – What would you like to accomplish today?

☐ Gratitude - What are you grateful for today?

TO DO LIST:

_____   _____

_____   _____

_____   _____

_____   _____

_____   _____

There are so many reasons to be happy today!

I am Grateful For:

_____

_____

_____

_____

_____

_____

_____

_____

_____

_____

_____

_____

_____

_____

_____

_____

_____

_____

_____

_____

"Gratitude makes sense of our past, brings peace for today, and creates a vision for tomorrow."

– Melody Beattie

REFLECTIONS:

<u>Daily Habits</u>

- ☐ Make your bed – First task of the day done!

- ☐ Drink a big glass of water – You've dehydrated while sleeping; quench your thirst!

- ☐ Stretch – Lengthen and loosen your body; it has been still for awhile!

- ☐ 5 minutes of physical activity – Get your blood pumping and your mind refreshed!

- ☐ 5 minutes of meditation – Focus on your breath and set your intentions for the day!

- ☐ Read for 5 minutes – Expand your knowledge!

- ☐ Make a 'To Do List' – What would you like to accomplish today?

- ☐ Gratitude - What are you grateful for today?

TO DO LIST:

_____	_____
_____	_____
_____	_____
_____	_____
_____	_____

If you can dream it, you can do it!

I am Grateful For:

_____

_____

_____

_____

_____

_____

_____

_____

_____

_____

_____

_____

_____

_____

_____

_____

_____

_____

_____

_____

_____

_____

Daily Habits

- ☐ Make your bed – First task of the day done!

- ☐ Drink a big glass of water – You've dehydrated while sleeping; quench your thirst!

- ☐ Stretch – Lengthen and loosen your body; it has been still for awhile!

- ☐ 5 minutes of physical activity – Get your blood pumping and your mind refreshed!

- ☐ 5 minutes of meditation – Focus on your breath and set your intentions for the day!

- ☐ Read for 5 minutes – Expand your knowledge!

- ☐ Make a 'To Do List' – What would you like to accomplish today?

- ☐ Gratitude - What are you grateful for today?

TO DO LIST:

_____   _____

_____   _____

_____   _____

_____   _____

_____   _____

The art of being happy is to be satisfied with what you have!

I am Grateful For:

_____

_____

_____

_____

_____

_____

_____

_____

_____

_____

_____

_____

_____

_____

_____

_____

_____

_____

_____

_____

_____

Daily Habits

☐ Make your bed – First task of the day done!

☐ Drink a big glass of water – You've dehydrated while sleeping; quench your thirst!

☐ Stretch – Lengthen and loosen your body; it has been still for awhile!

☐ 5 minutes of physical activity – Get your blood pumping and your mind refreshed!

☐ 5 minutes of meditation – Focus on your breath and set your intentions for the day!

☐ Read for 5 minutes – Expand your knowledge!

☐ Make a 'To Do List' – What would you like to accomplish today?

☐ Gratitude - What are you grateful for today?

TO DO LIST:

_____   _____

_____   _____

_____   _____

_____   _____

_____   _____

Enjoy the little things!

I am Grateful For:

_____

_____

_____

_____

_____

_____

_____

_____

_____

_____

_____

_____

_____

_____

_____

_____

_____

_____

_____

Daily Habits

☐ Make your bed – First task of the day done!

☐ Drink a big glass of water – You've dehydrated while sleeping; quench your thirst!

☐ Stretch – Lengthen and loosen your body; it has been still for awhile!

☐ 5 minutes of physical activity – Get your blood pumping and your mind refreshed!

☐ 5 minutes of meditation – Focus on your breath and set your intentions for the day!

☐ Read for 5 minutes – Expand your knowledge!

☐ Make a 'To Do List' – What would you like to accomplish today?

☐ Gratitude - What are you grateful for today?

TO DO LIST:

_____   _____

_____   _____

_____   _____

_____   _____

_____   _____

Be Strong; you never know who you are inspiring!

I am Grateful For:

_____

_____

_____

_____

_____

_____

_____

_____

_____

_____

_____

_____

_____

_____

_____

_____

_____

_____

_____

_____

_____

Daily Habits

☐ Make your bed – First task of the day done!

☐ Drink a big glass of water – You've dehydrated while sleeping; quench your thirst!

☐ Stretch – Lengthen and loosen your body; it has been still for awhile!

☐ 5 minutes of physical activity – Get your blood pumping and your mind refreshed!

☐ 5 minutes of meditation – Focus on your breath and set your intentions for the day!

☐ Read for 5 minutes – Expand your knowledge!

☐ Make a 'To Do List' – What would you like to accomplish today?

☐ Gratitude - What are you grateful for today?

TO DO LIST:

_____   _____

_____   _____

_____   _____

_____   _____

_____   _____

You are a Champion!!

I am Grateful For:

_____

_____

_____

_____

_____

_____

_____

_____

_____

_____

_____

_____

_____

_____

_____

_____

_____

_____

_____

Daily Habits

- [ ] Make your bed – First task of the day done!

- [ ] Drink a big glass of water – You've dehydrated while sleeping; quench your thirst!

- [ ] Stretch – Lengthen and loosen your body; it has been still for awhile!

- [ ] 5 minutes of physical activity – Get your blood pumping and your mind refreshed!

- [ ] 5 minutes of meditation – Focus on your breath and set your intentions for the day!

- [ ] Read for 5 minutes – Expand your knowledge!

- [ ] Make a 'To Do List' – What would you like to accomplish today?

- [ ] Gratitude - What are you grateful for today?

TO DO LIST:

_____   _____

_____   _____

_____   _____

_____   _____

_____   _____

Expect nothing, appreciate everything!

I am Grateful For:

_____
_____
_____
_____
_____
_____
_____
_____
_____
_____
_____
_____
_____
_____
_____
_____
_____
_____
_____
_____
_____
_____
_____

Daily Habits

☐ Make your bed – First task of the day done!

☐ Drink a big glass of water – You've dehydrated while sleeping; quench your thirst!

☐ Stretch – Lengthen and loosen your body; it has been still for awhile!

☐ 5 minutes of physical activity – Get your blood pumping and your mind refreshed!

☐ 5 minutes of meditation – Focus on your breath and set your intentions for the day!

☐ Read for 5 minutes – Expand your knowledge!

☐ Make a 'To Do List' – What would you like to accomplish today?

☐ Gratitude - What are you grateful for today?

TO DO LIST:

_____   _____

_____   _____

_____   _____

_____   _____

_____   _____

You've got this!!

I am Grateful For:

_____

_____

_____

_____

_____

_____

_____

_____

_____

_____

_____

_____

_____

_____

_____

_____

_____

_____

_____

_____

_____

_____

Daily Habits

☐ Make your bed – First task of the day done!

☐ Drink a big glass of water – You've dehydrated while sleeping; quench your thirst!

☐ Stretch – Lengthen and loosen your body; it has been still for awhile!

☐ 5 minutes of physical activity – Get your blood pumping and your mind refreshed!

☐ 5 minutes of meditation – Focus on your breath and set your intentions for the day!

☐ Read for 5 minutes – Expand your knowledge!

☐ Make a 'To Do List' – What would you like to accomplish today?

☐ Gratitude - What are you grateful for today?

TO DO LIST:

_____   _____

_____   _____

_____   _____

_____   _____

_____   _____

Don't forget to smile today!

I am Grateful For:

_____

_____

_____

_____

_____

_____

_____

_____

_____

_____

_____

_____

_____

_____

_____

_____

_____

_____

_____

_____

Daily Habits

☐ Make your bed – First task of the day done!

☐ Drink a big glass of water – You've dehydrated while sleeping; quench your thirst!

☐ Stretch – Lengthen and loosen your body; it has been still for awhile!

☐ 5 minutes of physical activity – Get your blood pumping and your mind refreshed!

☐ 5 minutes of meditation – Focus on your breath and set your intentions for the day!

☐ Read for 5 minutes – Expand your knowledge!

☐ Make a 'To Do List' – What would you like to accomplish today?

☐ Gratitude - What are you grateful for today?

TO DO LIST:

_____   _____

_____   _____

_____   _____

_____   _____

_____   _____

Live with purpose!!

I am Grateful For:

_____

_____

_____

_____

_____

_____

_____

_____

_____

_____

_____

_____

_____

_____

_____

_____

_____

_____

_____

_____

"*Acknowledging the good that you already have in your life is the foundation for all abundance*"

-Eckhart Tolle

REFLECTIONS:

"When I started counting my blessings, my whole life turned around"

-Willie Nelson

REFLECTIONS:

"*When you practice gratefulness, there is a sense of respect towards others*"

-Dalai Lama

REFLECTIONS:

"Without gratitude and appreciation for what you already have, you'll never know true fulfillment"

- Tony Robbins

Made in the USA
Las Vegas, NV
29 September 2022

56051625R00066